COMMENTS ON
PATRICIA NELSON & SPOKES OF DREAM AND BIRD

In the beginning, they say, was the word. Patricia Nelson, mistress of words that she is, is interested in what lies before that beginning. Was the invention of language, she seems to ask in some of her poems, entirely a gain? . . . . Again and again she zeroes in on the ways language can reduce experience, not do justice to it. Many of her poems feature those who abuse the language in some form. Orators, politicians, preachers come in for some bad reviews. They are shown using language to narrow things, limit things, draw lines that should not be drawn. . . . Nelson has great sympathy for the people—and creatures—that find themselves on the wrong side of the borders that words and analogous human powers create.
—John Hart, author of *The Climbers* and *Storm Camp*, co-editor of *Blue Unicorn*

◆ ◆ ◆

To read Patricia Nelson's poetry is to enter a vortex of language pushing you to a world that is sideways and awry. These hinted shapes breathe a tremendous vitality as each creature strives to "untwist the sky," and tell "a truth of salt and star." Patricia's touch can be deceptively light and gentle. But do not be lulled by the lovely "song that widens the mouth like a vowel"— read further and you may find "your red heart banging in its bowl."
—Jean Wong, author of *Sleeping with the Gods* and *Hurtling Jade and Other Tales of Personal Folly*

Patricia Nelson's poetry startles that mindspace where all known and well-worn thoughts live, scattering linguistic lodgepoles. Her words break open the familiar and pull us to the mumbling edge of unconscious recognition.
—Briahn Kelly-Brennan, poet

◆ ◆ ◆

In Spokes of Dream or Bird, Patricia Nelson reminds us again how words and things relate, and how sometimes they don't. For all that language is, for all it describes, shapes, enhances, and liberates, it remains discrete from its object, a pure label. In four parts, she explores "an old thought – like a small-footed spider." Proposing that dreaming is surfing waves to the shore, she challenges the very idea of the mind and its workings, its connection to language, and language's approximation of both subject and object. It's the best we can do, with poetry an apt translator. These are poems of thought, of the mysticism of the Druids, the symbolism of trees, the universality of Odysseus and his phantoms and phantasms, of dear ones lost, of permanence and impermanence, taking the stage quietly, in the shadows, "colors quiet in their jambs/edges understood."
—Jeff Santosuosso, poet, co-editor of *Panoply*, former co-editor of *Emerald Coast Review*

Spokes of Dream or Bird

Poems by Patricia Nelson

Poetic Matrix Press

ALSO BY PATRICIA NELSON

Among the Shapes That Fold & Fly, Sugartown Publishing, 2012

Cover design by Margaret Copeland.
Cover art by Saundra Kiehn.

ISBN: 978-0-9981469-4-2

Poetic Matrix Press
www.poeticmatrix.com

Acknowledgments

Grateful acknowledgment is made to the following publications in which these poems first appeared or will appear, sometimes in a slightly different form:

Weathers, in Avocet, 2012
Woman and Gulls and *Alder,* in Emerald Coast Review
    XVII, 2013
Oak, in U.S. 1 Worksheets, 2014
Dream, in the 2016 Marin Poetry Center Anthology
Sister Eulalia, Bernadine and *One Light,* in Stolen Light,
    the 2016 Redwood Writers Anthology
Willow, in Panoplyzine, 2016
Dragon and *Avenging Angels,* in The Listening Eye, 2017

Spokes of Dream or Bird
An Introduction to the poems of
Patricia Nelson

Expectations. What do we expect when we begin to read a poem? We may look for the familiar, the images and metaphors that we associate with poetry. We may expect some kind of form, of rhyme or partial rhyme. We may look for subjects that we associate with poetry—love, perhaps, and certainly loss. We may look for the familiar in landscapes that we know. We may look for a contemporized mythic element, if we are so disposed. We may look for aspects of ourselves.

When you pick up a book by Patricia Nelson, be prepared for your expectations to be, at first, subtly met. It is the language of poetry. It looks like poems you have read. You begin to relax. Then, you find yourself stopped, in your tracks, as it were. What is going on? What has she done to your expectations? If you are like me, you go back to the beginning. You start over. You begin to realize you are on the cusp of poetry, a dimension of poetry rarely experienced. You begin again, more slowly this time, savoring the power of a master poet.

When I first encountered Pat Nelson's poems, I was, frankly, stunned. Here they were; they looked like poems. They sounded like poems. But they turned my expectations totally around. Here was language used at the edge of its meanings. Here was myth turned into a new kind of reality. Here was a new knowledge of what it means to use language in a way that forces us as readers to come to a new understanding of the conjunctions of images that force us to see the world in a new way.

I know more now. I know that Pat Nelson is one of the new Activists, but knowing and having worked with one of the originators of Activism, I see her work taking yet a bold new direction, one that quietly forges new ways of looking at the environment, of looking at ancient texts in completely contemporary ways, of shaking up our expectations of what poetry is, what it can be, what it must be in this new world.

—Fran Claggett, poet, teacher, author of three books of poetry and fifteen books on the teaching and assessing of writing; writer and consultant to *Education and the Economy*

Contents

Spokes of Dream or Bird

The Word That Countersigns

After Fire, Alder First: Trees and Other Archetypes

AFTER DANTE: INFERNO

EXITS AND ENTRANCES

ABOUT THE AUTHOR

PREFACE
THE "ACTIVISTS" ARE BACK

Or, more precisely, we're still here. This San Francisco Bay Area group, which first gathered around Lawrence Hart in the 1930s, achieved a number of prestigious awards and a period of national recognition in the 1940s and 50s. The Activists experienced several decades of near invisibility as a different style, less wedded to technique and more focused on raw emotion and political rebellion, took center stage in the 1960s. However, they continued to meet and write in the background, publishing sporadically. Recently, a new generation of Activists has raised the flag again with a surge in publications displaying the characteristic Activist style.

In view of their history, currently only a few people know who the Activists are or what they stand for. The Activists are a group of poets defined by their use of a specific set of skills taught first by Lawrence and then by his son, poet John Hart. Lawrence's first group of students called themselves Activists because they were attempting to make every word in their poems aesthetically active via a common set of poetic tools. The adoption of this name predated the present political connotation.

Lawrence met this first and best-recognized group of students when he began teaching adult extension classes under a New Deal program. These students included Jeanne McGahey, Rosalie Moore, and Robert Horan. He went on to teach students of all kinds and all ages in a career that extended from the 1930s to the 1990s. Unlike many proselytizing teachers, Lawrence did not require that you share his politics or other beliefs, that you belong to an "elite" subset of students, or even that he liked you personally. If you indicated any interest in mastering a demanding set of poetry skills, that was enough to earn you his best teaching efforts.

The mission of the group that Lawrence gathered around himself was to systematically mine the complex new poetic territory that the Modernist poets had opened up. He fashioned a series of exercises that he believed would enable any willing apprentice to begin to master the effects he admired in the Modernists, who were still rather recent arrivals on the poetry scene when Lawrence began teaching.

Lawrence launched his teaching process by demanding that his initially flummoxed students "just report" what comes to their senses, leaving out all of the easy adjectives and generalizations. An exercise that is, of course, so much harder than it sounds. Lawrence did not let up until the student was free of all trite comparisons and had also learned to recognize the details that are sharp and interesting and that recreate a sensory experience, a pattern of awareness in the reader's mind.

He then introduced us to metaphoric imagery and related organizational skills. He asked the student to combine two disparate objects, using their "shadow meanings" or connotations to create a new and intense unit of meaning. Borrowing from the musical concept of balancing accord and discord, and citing Henry Lanz, Lawrence suggested that poetic excitement does not come from an immediate sense of pleasure but rather from a gradual sense of recognition. He observed that unusual combinations of objects in an image or other poetic notation might be not at all pleasing on first encounter. The unusual is often both surprising and discordant. To satisfy the reader aesthetically, the discord must be balanced by an accord—a feeling of pleasure, excitement, or a sense of the rightness in what is said or the way of saying it.

One example Lawrence liked to cite is e. e. cummings' image, "a water-smooth silver stallion." Water and a horse: an unexpected combination that, on reflection, accurately describes the qualities of a galloping stallion. Cummings draws out the pleasant sensory associations common to the two objects; the words "smooth" and "silver" accord the surprising combination. They bring to mind the coat and color of a particular horse as well as its gait and a rippling of muscle. They make the description pleasurable as well as true to the experience of watching the horse.

Never one to shrink from a challenge, Lawrence encouraged his students to reach for the most unusual combinations we were able to accord. He introduced the further organizational technique of a "connotative line" in which the side meanings of a series of strong images are picked up and reinforced from line to line, creating a consistent sense of awareness. Finally, "connotative statement" moves away from image and into the realm of ideas, but seeks to retain the dual sense of surprise and accuracy that is found in a good image.

Lawrence did not invent the set of skills he taught so persistently. Rather, he distilled what he observed and appreciated in Modernist poetry and then tried to reverse-engineer the ways in which the Modernists achieved these effects. Just as he was succeeding, the times changed, a new style asserted itself, and the attention of readers seemed to dissipate. Lawrence declared war on the new style, objecting that a vast and promising new territory for poets was being abandoned before it had been fully assimilated. History seems to say that Lawrence lost that war.

There were always certain obstacles for poets using the Modernist/Activist techniques. Even in the heyday of the Modernists, many readers were not prepared to accept discord as a poetic value. And the Activist practice of closely packing a line with challenging images struck some readers as "too much." One might expect that the current generation of Activist poets would experience a higher degree of resistance or indifference.

Our experiences vary because we are each taking the Activist techniques "out into the world" again in our own different ways. In presenting my work in non-Activist writing groups where we have time to listen carefully to each other, I have not experienced the hostility or resistance that might be expected in a "war" of poetic styles. There are some people who "take to" the Activist techniques right away and want to learn how to use them. There are some who comment, probably accurately, "If I wrote that way for the markets that publish me, I would be excommunicated." And in one response that I found oddly heartening, one very fine poet said, "I used to always wonder what she was talking about, but the recent poems seem completely clear. I don't know if her work has changed or if I've changed."

Each book in the recent resurgence of Activist publications stands or falls on its own merits, of course. But each is also, in part, a kind of testimony that the territory Lawrence charted so carefully is still vital and interesting and has something to contribute to poetry. The ability to appreciate this "something" depends a great deal on significant exposure to the style.

Patricia Nelson
San Rafael, CA
May 2017

Activist Books of Poetry
- Spokes of Dream or Bird, by Patricia Nelson,
    Poetic Matrix Press 2017
- Storm Camp, by John Hart, Sugartown 2017
- Sun on the Rind, by Bonnie Thomas, Sugartown 2015
- At My Table, by Judith Yamamoto, Sugartown 2014
- It Lasts a Moment (New & Collected Poems), by
    Fred Ostrander, Sugartown 2013
- Among the Shapes That Fold & Fly, by Patricia
    Nelson, Sugartown 2012
- Petroglyphs, by Fred Ostrander, Blue Light Press 2009
- Gutenberg at Strasbourg, by Rosalie Moore,
    Floating Island Press 1995
- Homecoming with Reflections, by Jeanne McGahey,
    Quarterly Review of Literature 45th Anniversary
    Edition 1989
- Blue Holes, by Laurel Trivelpiece, Alice James Books 1987
- Of Singles and Doubles, by Rosalie Moore, Woolmer
    Brotherson 1979
- The Climbers, by John Hart, Pitt Poetry Series 1978
- The Hunchback and the Swan, by Fred Ostrander,
    Woolmer Brotherson 1978
- Legless in Flight, by Laurel Trivelpiece, Woolmer
    Brotherson 1978
- Alleluia Chorus, by Lois Moyles, Woolmer Brotherson
    1978
- Year of the Children: Poems for a Narrative, by
    Rosalie Moore, Woolmer Brotherson 1977
- Oregon Winter, by Jeanne McGahey, Woolmer
    Brotherson 1973
- I Prophesy Survivors, by Lois Moyles, Woolmer
    Brotherson 1971
- Accent on Barlow poems by Robert Barlow and other
    Activist poets], published by Lawrence Hart 1962

·The Grasshopper's Man and Other Poems, by
Rosalie Moore, Yale Younger Poets Series 1949
·A Beginning, by Robert Horan, Yale Younger Poets
Series 1948
·Five Young American Poets [with poems by Jeanne
McGahey], New Directions 1941
·Mid-Day at Calydon, by Rosalie Moore, Charles
Sergel Award for verse drama, University of
Chicago 1938

DEDICATION

For the Harts, Lawrence and John and Jeanne McGahey,
and my colleagues in the Hart seminars. Thanks also to my
more recent poetry colleagues in Terry Ehret's Sitting Room
workshops and the "Monday poets" group led by Fran
Claggett and Jean Wong. Further thanks to John Peterson
of Poetic Matrix Press for taking a chance on this work.

SPOKES OF DREAM OR BIRD

The Word That Countersigns

WOMAN AND GULLS

The woman walks among the gulls.
Around her hand, the gathered:
strident, airborne, eyed.
Hand moves, cries move.

Yellow mouths grab
angles of bread,
sky, accelerating wind,
grab the moment
turning sideways into absence.

She cannot touch the word that countersigns
the perpetual resounding want
beaked and hooked
and thrown always into a wind.

BELOW

How do you say the light,
the tree loud in its flying maze
of stem and bird?
And below, the quiet seam,
awry and caught.

How do you say the hive
with its spiral of bees,
rift of small live faces moving?
And below, the wild voices dark,
piled like rocks.

Where do they go
and how do you say it all,
with voices short as shadows
and the knocking derrick of a phrase
above the still and mineral understory?

EXPLAINING

In the silence
her face stops slowly
as a bell.

She looks away,
leaves like comment
her eye's white corner.

Begins to explain,
widens the top of her hand.
Smallness of skin
caught on a shape of water.

O feel come down on its thread
the old thought like a small-footed spider.

Explaining disclaims the oddities
(the low, indifferent moon,
the shadow self, its unintended color
of cannon or headline)
and tries to own.

STATEMENT

(David, a stutterer)

i.
I must live in the lamplight squall
of blameless angry mouths
whose words arrive together and alight.

Words without bruise,
waxed words bright as furniture,
tawdry in their curve and shine.

Each face alive at cheek and eye
Suggesting with unbroken words correctness:
A whole with a space and a plan.

An indoor truth.

ii.
I must speak in smaller words.
So much wind between the thoughts,
so much loud ocean at the outlet pushing back.

Mine——the white forms gusting
in a sack around my skull,
so close the moon's edge stings like paper.

My face chalked by the leaning surf of morning,
I untwist the sky, let out the hard
unlovely shapes, the pale ones flying.

Wild words: A truth of salt and star.

SERENA

For the strong, some sins are impersonal.
My sins, the pale sins of the weak:
Deferential lie, the forfeit.
Little glimmer of receding face,
bowl painted white and raised to others.

The strong make a mark where the faint slide under.
Remember the bog that singed the footing,
forget the ones that they pushed down.
The wrong, if any, is small,
and the gods avenging little wrongs long gone.

But like faces folded by their colors
the lie evacuates toward knowledge.
The lost find the wilderness of the eye,
the air of the reconsidered word.
The curve, the motion.

The mechanism always rolls
its shunts and screws:
alters those who were strong
or right
or simply there.

BERNADINE
(A writer of fictions)

I live in the quiet place
circled by a father's rage.
I find the shadowed chairs,
a refugee of few and oddly ironed words.

My face, on its minor stem, is moving:
named in greeting widens like a mouth
a flowering doorway, lighted room;
named otherwise it flickers and recedes.

I live in the nuance—the light
most alive at the half-shape.
Here the not-yet stammers its shape
like moonlight folded oddly on a shoulder.

I will someday sing, and sting
the many loudnesses—
the tall and stamping hero
and the silence he requires.

I will write the people singing,
the objects that they swing two-handed:
Barrels, dowels, bags of onions,
objects rolling in their own sounds.

I will write the river,
among stones its many odd names,
moving the sliding, biting creatures,
until all is seen and recollected.

I will write the self, turned seaward
like a dye that resuspends and redeposits
until it owns its poison and its shape.
I will say finally:

How bent by sunlight is the shadow that we make.

DREAM

A word, a father's light, a shape on water
coincidence to move and shine and fold.
Dream it shoreward: image, breakage, daughter.
A face that floats in circle, edge, and cold.

The loud and literal walk upon a shadow,
a story with an incremental space
a wave that breaks the color in the shallows.
In dream all water will unwind a face.

Who rides the slanted wish will fall from air
and see the glaring image riding him.
The disregarded face will reappear
the omitted widen like a broken hem.

Dreams migrate to a shore where colors part
and clear and dark repeat the waiting heart.

SISTER EULALIA

Around me are the heart-high boys
a spill of circles, shadows.
At their level—noise, gust, grab,
pigeons swinging the unguided, windy colors.

What do they know of tall garments,
small grammatical eyes,
blue eyes that move and gather—
that will change them?

You, boy, at the verge of my voice and shadow,
walk your cruel extravagant bag of organs
to the brink, extinct and falling outward. Come here!

I have sailed around
the rocks I see, the hungers I know.
Far behind, the famine, the landlords
A mark on ocean thinner than my upraised child-arm.

I came in a slipping foundering skin.
I brought a will and a God,
a self to pocket like a muttering shell.
I read, I remembered, I extracted.

You, boy, walking glyph for "vessel,"
an object to fill or voyage with an object.
(To sacrifice is to make holy.) See where I will take you!

Always words and intonations to be made useful,
numbers—little black fish to hook and marshal.
And he who owns the table
owns the words.

So many at the future's edge like awls and shovels,
foreigners with oddly folded vowels,
children bent forward as if walking uphill,
children tilted back and looking up, as if resting in a
    boat. So many!

You, Mr. Mayor, who told you to read Aquinas,
to pinch your nose at night so it won't turn up?
The scholar's path exacts, wears deeper as it soars.

I pluck out the lucky, the industrious,
tell them how to get to Heaven and the right rooms.
Salvation is to stand in a bright light—
reflecting your Creator. *You, boy, approach the water, the*
communion.

Water slides among rocks
mutters like the man acquiring his reputation.
Baptism of power indirect,
wide and loud at the curve.

Many years on, in the right rooms,
my boys and no others.
Asked who they remember, what they did right,
they remember me, and they do right!

WE STAND

We stand, when we love, at an old sill,
the first thought still to overtake,
to widen a face upon the loved.

We can't go past the famished eye,
can't sound out the dazzle of lines,
the smile of words that embed and exonerate.

Virtues vanish, whiteness into wave
swallowed and swallowers of light
and there is only what we want:

The resonant antagonist
who takes us with small lamps
to the audible, uncanny light.

ONE LIGHT

Here is one light,
one sea
with one noise,
hunting the edge.

The storm, mechanical
as fastened stars,
turns landward
on its shrieking threads.

The woman at her table
with circles of water,
implements two-sided and silver,
folds stillness and shadow.

Turns with her eyes the blowing colors,
the driftwood's moteless rolling,
the colored planets that can't help
the way they spin.

One space gestures and flickers,
one sky of color and noise.
No word for another light
and no Word.

AFTER FIRE, ALDER FIRST:
TREES AND OTHER ARCHETYPES

ALDER

Alder is a tree sacred to the Druids, whose alder pipes gave rise to the legend of whistling up the wind. Alder is also a pioneer tree after fire, colonizing the stream's edge.

After fire, alder first,
edgewise in the earth.
In air and water, two shapes move,
a hail of surface, angle, leaf.

Wood of bridge and flute,
dwells in the flooded naked edge
where air in the green wood
makes a sound and shape.

From stream and air
pull with wood the elements.
Let wind pass through the tool
lifted like a thumb or moon.

A man goes single, finned with magic
through the raining, sliding air.
Colors beat in the sky
like flying animals.

The veined man ringing in the wind
sings to wing and eye and notch of leaf,
each small motion
and its many shadows.

Oak

The Druids saw the oak as a dimension door and considered it sacred. Druids and priestesses entered the future by listening to the oak leaves and wrens in the branches.

As the white ear carries the song away,
as starlight twists in the branch until it is gone,
so the door of the oak goes dark
and bird and leaf begin to move.

There is light adrift in the dark,
sift of bright grain in a wheel.
A chaff of noises
winnowed in the ear's small, shifting sea.

The human words are small and random,
easily forgotten, broken in the wall.
But the door of the oak is fierce with music,
sings to the woman's slant and branching awe.

The priestess widens at the door,
her flowering, altering map,
her Vision, large on its little hinge.
Her birded air and roaring star.

FIR

Fir is a tall slender tree that grows in high places.
Fir signifies high views and long sights with a clear
vision of what is beyond and yet to come.

Like spokes of dream or bird,
fir ravels into sky
its thin and calling colors.

Watcher, both dream and bird,
narrow as air in a spire,
arrows out to the revolving, delving sea.

Watcher, lacking error,
speaks in small, high words,
breathes into the clear a point of terror.

Eye in the lit face sees
horizons of thorn-sharp shapes, the loved ship,
not tranquil, on the folding, altering sea.

WILLOW

The Celts considered willow groves magical
and associated the willow with water, healing,
inspiration and the granting of wishes. They tied
a willow limb in a knot when making a wish.

This is the grove for wishing:
river's whispering sill,
joint of root and water,
green that shines and breathes.

White mist slurs the lost
men who rest on knee and heel,
faces winged with paints,
each man with a knot of words.

In wild, pliant verbs, they speak the edge.
Faces, downward in the air,
upward on the water,
join the elements that twist and whisper.

Among the edges loosening their heels
and water's legless, drifting animals,
go the headlong men who wish,
abandoned to the small and several things that sting.

They go far, go fast,
bend like water at the steep stone,
fold their known and disappearing sky
and may outlast the dry and footed men.

ELDER

The elder tree is the emblem of the 13th month in the Celtic calendar, the line between beginning and end. The elder is associated with witches, who live in the tree or ride its branches, and with pipes. Legend says that if you fall asleep under an elder tree, you will see into the world of the faeries.

The year flickers and recedes.
Horizon sifts and darkens,
drags a weight of stars
to a beginning or an end.

World of obsidian, eye of opal.
Woman thin in a night sky
shines at eye and buckle.
Bleeds at break of branch or ritual.

Her tree is small and crooked,
white at bud, dark at berry. It holds all:
black wing, flower's slow white beat,
winds she turns like a noise of horse.

Old Mother moves in her little bent tree
as music occupies a flute
or sweetness finds the hole of the hive
with the many striped and lisping skins of bees.

Do not use her without prayer
for wood or tool or fire.
Do not sleep in the loop of her shadow,
her minor blowing rim of dream.

She might sentence you to stay, to know,
with your little black eye and wailing shadow,
some trick of time or music.
Some snag of faerie at your false and cloth-bright world.

Or she might turn you to stone
at the verge, the violent silver verge
of whatever win you were leaning toward
over your moon-colored horse and crescent sword.

Rowan

*In legend, the tree from which the first woman
was made, and sacred to the goddess. The "tree
of life" and a tree of vision, with bright red berries.
It can survive at high altitudes and in seemingly
impossible places.*

From places high and cold and odd
from small bleak holes
ride the whispering tree.

Thin by thin, by rock or river,
a sheaf of bird and weather
down the cliff in wide and windy bud.

Rowan speaks to eye and pulse;
Her berries shake in an outer world
the womb's round color.

First Woman makes a shape,
steps sidelong through her door,
vision and redder, brighter vision.

O tree of charm and sign,
see, go by the hunters' quiet eye
of shine and slipping skin.

See it widen like an animal or child.
See it catch the tall and other world
in the sudden bag of a thought.

Tree, incant in sounds of silk or paper
all the hushed worlds fallen like snow,
stopped short in a sound.

BIRCH

The birch is the tree of the first month in the Celtic calendar. It is associated with the moon, birth and renewal, purification. Birch is a pioneer tree that renews the landward areas of a forest destroyed by fire or clear-cutting.

Remember the hoof-bright moons
that came in a hail of days.
Those were days that turned and clattered
and carried the greedy into the forest.

The forest thornless and unmaimed
before and after the ruin of now.
A furious, still moon stays over it
like a white barking.

How far is it to the rebirth,
the round light strengthening like a voice?
Know the distance by the size of the light
that widens like a pale root.

Silver light, your stem, your circle
where the doorway sleeps like a new animal.
Make the cloth of details
the death and the burning.

Any rebirth is hard, newborn muscle
twisting in its freedom.
Recalled only in dream like a white door moving
or a long-armed swimmer pale in the green of the water.

Make this wood hoop to sing through.
Make the moment not a moment.

APPLE

In a loop of shine and color
a woman with an apple.
She turns the words, the circle.

The apple in its weight
is cooler than her palm.
Her thumb slows and widens at the curves.

Three brown holes and a shape
of shadow on the apple
and some knowledge under the color.

It sounds like a cello.
It smells like blackberries.
It is whiter than an ocean wave.

Weathers

In doctrine a place of air,
a Church.
Each word an aisle
annexed to the next.
Each lung at its prayer
moving, audible, gleaning.

Colors quiet in their jambs,
edges understood.
To and fro the voices fold and open,
books of tiny weathers,
distinctions always smaller,
smaller, smaller

Against the loud and black and thrashing,
outside omnivorous indifferent storm.
Storm swallowed by
and swallower of destination.
A map unheard, unwanted.
A crash fastened to the light.

Hero

Is he true, that far thing
with words and hair,
solid shape
that stops hand and eye
and nothing else?

He rides a thistle of light.
He is a thing set off
to alter toward some cliff,
clear star broken by a crooked eye,
a trick of air or distance.

He is a set of edges,
temporary
on our flowering, altering maps.
Disaster turning in a battle,
a song that widens the mouth like a vowel.

Oh let him stay,
or let him falter
somewhere else,
not too close
or too real.

VIKINGS

Somewhere else, not here,
lies the dream and blue silence
where old things open easily.

Here are the shouldered, weighted men,
widest, coldest at the armor,
upright on a line of rock and ocean.

They hold totems: bone with a singe of shadow,
candle with its inch of light
moving, leaning seedwise.

In weather, fast as pinecones,
the warriors somehow clearer, better
for the knives of air and shadow.

They are singing on an edge
with hinges
known and aching like a jaw.

They dream a calm blue place
where variations on a line are small,
speak gently to the hand like cups and bells.

AFTER DANTE: INFERNO

THE ROAD
After Dante: Inferno Canto 1

i.
Enter with your trinket word
where colors open upward urgently as birds
and the wish for the mountain sings
as if it faces forward.

Pull from the dream the images of peak and tree.
Open their lamps among the windy surfaces,
the scarred and tangled maps
that are yours.

Starting at the middle, nudge a disappearing path.
Where the way is broken, you must break,
stippled pilgrim with your heel upon your shadow
and the wood's shadow.

ii.
The traveler begins,
knot of dreams like a lumbering animal,
image in the labyrinth,
distraction multiplied and sung.

The traveler sees his end,
the far, cold, indifferent mountain,
the power to stop among the lights
apart from the animals,

And every dark that roars
and turns below the prayer.

AT THE GATES OF HELL

Here, disjointed from a reputation,
my words have lost their handles;
I am blind and still.
In a language full of undertow
I have no weight but silence
and I fall in a dream without gavel.

Here, adrift, I would recall the nymphs,
in a night full of moon
as a dreamer stammers half-formed insects.
I would call back the other silhouettes,
white and without excess,
and the single outline that discerns and loves.

In the world I walked among the days,
towers tolled in long and several ways.
Their pattern came to me at last,
distilled from time and rock and water.
The line I drew myself with repetition:
Echo, mirror, window.

After life, I am bent with dead words.
I step through the baying gate,
rise by falling, step among the errors.
The blue lift of the little flower,
the stone bud of the mountain.
It is heavy, a foretaste of rising.

THE RIVER

Here the damned wait, without cry or slander.
No savior comes, no hero rises.
They drop their leaking bundle of laws,
their sheaf of spotted crimes.

They wear their acts only, their faces
where a white light flies like paper.
All they own is the hour, turning,
the impersonal end with its flowering odor of lion.

The hour pulls us tight around them:
Reflection or refrain.
Called by the skin of their acts,
we stand out of world, ajar.

GUIDE

As if you twitch a music slowly
on your four moving fingers,
oh, please make number of this sagging light
and of this wish of mine enlarging like a fine.

I want to see it all,
slide past the ogre
in his place between the aches,
long and deaf as a bone.

Oh guide, not sent for me,
still I hear you red and sifting in my ear.
I am in the burnt and sung place
and like the other sinners I must buy my voice.

THE PILGRIM

What can a pilgrim do in Hell
but watch with sandstone eye
as men fall through the cold, dishonored circles,
the tundra colors,
the record's many mineral collars.

One ungainly question flowers
in the whitened rolling faces:
What is the end and the falsity.
Retribution: that calm monster
with the sleeping paw and crocus eye.

The ignoble climb at last
the circle of the stairs.
They find with eye and palm
the many empty spaces—
put hands to the collapsing stars.

Pilgrim: stare and stand
below the story's mountain,
thirsting.
With no water in your hand,
your wishbone of dry air.

THE SINNERS IN HELL STILL HAVE THEIR BODIES

i.
The sinners arrive, many and hard to move.
They are heavy, utilitarian
as sandbags or big herbivores.
They are eating
the collective weather.

Uneasy in an abstract thunder
each stands also in his single storm
and the death his storm dropped, at last,
on an indifferent surface
and a lack of time.

In his ringing body
one still thinks the falling water,
dissonant and hard, is potable.
But his eye holds nothing
starless and dry.

His body, when asked what it is,
holds up the sack of its wants,
the paper sigh of its first language.
Remembers how it came here calling,
in its bag of pulse and noise.

ii.
The sinners have a function here.
They ease the devil's loneliness.
They darken the empty rings around him
drop with elbows outward, knocking.

And they disappoint him
with their obvious, compiled sins,
their bodies the color of water
and water the shape of nothing.

They drag stinging predictable skin,
cries and wishes. In their pain
they think no terror larger than their terror,
no love more lost.

PAOLO AND FRANCESCA

*Dante finds Paolo and Francesca in a whirlwind
in the second circle of Hell, in which they are
punished for the unrepented sin of lust. Francesca
was the mistress of Paolo, her husband's brother,
who killed them both on discovering their affair.*

Tell your story to the traveler
from the living world.
One who has lover he can't touch
and a wife who will not kill.

Tell how the face without conventions
flies its reddened leaf.
Its veins bird-wide
on a water long with images.

Say you thought to ride the horses riding you,
the light alive everywhere it touches you.
See your love in every burning shape:
Flower, sun, covered worded page.

Stand at the same sill. Forever.
Call the one that you wish to see into.
Throw into a dazzle your wishing coin,
your round and singing sin.

You stand undeterred in Hell
by the cool tall watcher.
Roll your story without thought
into the light that cartwheels after him.

THE SUICIDES

In the Inferno, the suicides appear as trees in a
barren forest, in a circle of Hell that punishes the
sin of violence. After the Judgment, they will hold
their dead earthly bodies on their branches.

i.
In the forest one face live, and many dead
moan loss in colors violent and wrong.
Trees shaved of bird and motion
exhale permanence and weight and volume.

Heavy, the still, stone-colored dead,
on their root, knuckled into ground.
The far stiff men who lean with wind and stem
are marked like branches with the dark directions.

They are twisting in their wood
dream garishly of thorn and harpy.
They who drew with provisional bodies
the irrevocable sin.

ii.
The living watcher comes in his unspotted odor
watertight and white as roses. And proud.
Unlike the tall dead faces
loud with accurate holes of eye and mouth.

Around and through the real,
the watcher winds the words for real,
compounds the wound,
sums the maimed fruit.

But oh, the place he comes from, ignorant and worded,
with iridescent bird
and time to reconsider colors like silk in the wind
and a moving knee and shoulder.

ULYSSES IN HELL

Dante tells a unique story of Ulysses' last voyage, in which he sailed away from home and family in his old age and drowned with his crew within sight of the mountain of Purgatory.

i.

In old age, he laid it down again,
the adventure like a gamble
his ship, mast dwindling upward into light.
on the flat and singing sea.

He rode the fate that once had shone and slid
around him like a water, rolling its odd images.
He went out past the edge,
sailing like a stub among the bigger, brighter gods.

Escaped those who loved and kept him small
and satisfied. And yes, he did come upon,
like a mirror or a minor shadow,
the vast, upward mountain of the saved.

But here he lost. The turning sea: the answer.
Like the horn that winds the sound in circles
until it is loud and bright and final—it pulled him down.
Pulled him down at last into the refrain of who he is.

Drowned him with his old and striving gods—
who love the sly thief, the merely smart escape,
love the brave and presumptuous—
who blow and tap the world like a drunken orchestra.

ii.
The favored watcher makes a story
of the sunken hero twisting without volume,
baffled form moving as if splashing,
the loss still diving.

Makes an exit straight and dim as starlight
where all the blue ghosts leave,
the path around them
closing like a seam.

Men bone-colored and still,
women off-key in their hanging shapes,
no longer in that fiction
where the place can change.

UGOLINO

*In the 9th circle of Hell, Dante finds Count Ugolino,
a power-seeking nobleman who has repeatedly
betrayed his political allies. His enemies finally
locked him in a tower with his small sons and
grandsons, and left all of them to starve. As they
are dying, the children lovingly invite Ugolino to
eat them, an invitation he accepts.*

This is not the room I meant,
not this rim of fallen sons
withering beside my sinking elbow.
Not this hunger or this sacrifice
fastened to a barking of walls
and a new darkness wailing like a city.

I meant to be believed
when I set before so many others
their dishonored exit like a small candle.
I had not meant to be audible,
not seen to be pulled upward
by my hunger.

Oh my little princes
who offered me their bones!
They rest in the air around me, mark it like a glyph.
They go to a place that I will never see.
Blessed princes, carved for a better fate
than the one that darkens like a stain around me.

The many allies I unfastened
have now unfastened me,
have left me in this circle waning like a lamp.
My mouth balloons at the injustice.
Oh I am blind
still and always!

AVENGING ANGELS

At the crack in the world,
the starved crack in the world,
are the narrow angels.
In black air the thin, suspended angels.

With silver hands and eyes they search
the shining, slipping waters,
like the striking mouths of fish.
With knife-colored wing they revise flesh.

You must part from the animals,
the dark and crying roses of their mouths.
You must drown upward,
you who know nothing of rising.

Ask at the opening for light
and hear the bellowing dark. The rescuers
from whom you hope to escape
with your minor ropes and ladders.

Ask, ask, with the flying ovals of your hands.

EXITS AND ENTRANCES

DRAGON

i.
Dragon slides from the dark,
the nimbus of grey rock
the hole of light in his mountain.

He goes hot where the fear sings,
Neck of shine and scale moving,
curve upon curve, among the winds.

His mouth widens its circle.
Its heart of red stars, billowing,
its bellow of burning iron.

The dragon eye comes
down, askew and round,
near to the hero's eye.

The hero's eye is still,
small and blank as a thumb,
and far from magic.

ii.
The two circle, knee and shoulder,
before the fight begins to growl and twist
and only one is small and full of cold.

Courage comes and courage goes
in what sky and on what back,
in what new red heart banging in its bowl.

No light, no spell forgets
the many times that courage came before
and nothing after.

Still it comes again with tools in air,
a little wind of blade or word,
alive for now and resting on a breath.

SHADOWS

Who is it makes the shadow,
cool and sliding spill
that captures crack and elbow,
those things dropped, alive in a different wind.

Thicker than the space he stands on,
the man bends his shadow.
On the sill of light
he draws a headlong shape.

He looks through bone and skin
at what is similar and distant.
With one hand touches shape—
edge, and grasses that move the edge.

He moves the dark.
Speaks the wave,
the gull in its blueward line,
the hand at the edge of strangeness.

In his words is something moving like the leaf
the wing in the fraying worm.
His face says "not so strange"
the bright and flying skin with its new eye.

ADAM AND EVE EXPELLED

They, avoiding the final disaster,
take up again their lack of doubt.
They see at last—Here they will take it all
with sentient, aching muscles,
shapes alive at the elbows.

Like the first among the flowers,
they interrogate the cold,
the crocodile weather,
with the black and slapdash tail;
ask again at the little den with its fold of bear.

They do not see the God behind them
or the slant ambiguous absence.
They do not fear the sky with rolling planets,
jibbing, booming visitations
among the spiral, crane-colored stars.

Here they are in the region of their importance,
with the noisy shapes of their wants around them,
almost familiar, almost appropriate, like children.
Here they sing and shake their weapons,
make on their maps their flowering, altering shadow.

Their faces with the folded eyes
hold all the creatures, odd and calling.
They are oval, they are water,
they are moving.
Death in the folded eye.

Not Eden

Here there is no edge and no landmark:
There is only "outside,"
where winds revise away the sand at our heels.

Here we step with care
among the dry, ticking rocks,
the quickening of snake and dust.

Here we follow the pot-colored sun
and we carry the heavy blood in lines
under the skin, metallic and banging.

We see the animals, already named,
with space and heat between them,
superb and drying in their colors. Apart.

Not Yet

We who enter rattle the moment,
Sing the door that finds us—
new, miraculous, our hands wide
on the world's original, meant shape.

We are inside now,
armed with skin and shadow,
an alphabet of bone and tool
to mine the rocks and silences.

> Look: Cold comes sidelong,
> something caught.
> Shine is noisy
> where the fish come out.

And still we ring and turn, apart.
Tongues swing in their chinks
as if recalling the exception.
The family's little line of eyes forgives.

> One day, where sun
> goes small across a bowl of shadows,
> across our old faces in the photos,
> powdered and persistent as moths,
> someone will close the light.

But for now, only in dreams
does water pull apart our twig-dark shapes.

> Not yet, the small, hard, heeling steps,
> the burn of likeness.

THE THING DISLODGED
(After a death)

O your face, your lamplit face
and all the faces loose like leaves
in the cold black wind.
Do not turn back—the falling
turning world is fastened to your skin.

With only sound or water in your hand,
believe the river widens at its end.
Your eye collects the twist of bright, blowing surfaces,
infers escape, the leaning talon of the sail,
as if the thing dislodged implies a place to land.

Do not repent the vision,
large, erroneous and shared;
or the voyage, singular and hard,
the scant and canted signs,
the far, pulling, iron stars.

Infer horizon, a spilled circle and an end,
a skin that flattens shoreward like a wave
a silence uttered somewhere else.
The same word always left behind,
the tall, grave, singing word for more.

When One Who is Loved is Gone

What to make of all
the sediments and angles,
the heart's alluvial inks?
The arriving anger
and all its squirming paints?

The words of lime
and eyes of chalk,
the stile collapsing
like the parchment bones.

In the loss are loosened worms.
They roll in the dark like brushes, wanting sight.
They disturb the pouches of the earth,
the grinding weights
where the spool of fire is pressed out.

As if in another place,
the words accrete as gradually as ointments.
Revise the flailing picture left to heal
on a flat and howling surface.

SOMETHING RESOUNDS

Yellow and indirect
wider at the curve
the planets come down.
They cover the ground
in faint, far circles
without sound or odor.

Something resounds
in the leaf-fall of shapes
the language of accidents.
Something in the words that turn
in the ear's small folding seas.
A wish that rolls and steams and burns.

There is a moment
still turning in its first shape.
It sends our faces riding
colors small and temporary
to the farthest minute.
We know it through its pane of weather.

Ulysses

What do they see,
those travelers lost and constantly in motion?
They see all the holes for resting,
random as caves, and as innocent.
But dangerous.

Those who wander come to think
that they have made the cave.
Or changed it in their sleep,
eyes turned backward, sleeved and calculating,
like the pulsing face of a watch.

In the dark, the wanderer must think of home
like the curb he steps from, twitching,
At the edge of sleep,
he dreams home falsely
in the shadow shapes of rest.

Those resting never see
the real shape of rest,
its deeps, its tenants
swinging jaw and wing
singing eye-shaped sailors onto sea.

COLLECTORS

Does it call to you, the future
where the offense you really meant
is pardoned—a noise torn and mixed with air
like the crude map of the conquered or the child?

Stubborn in your defects, you had few collectors.
You drove words like stakes to mark the shadows.
Your guiding moon a place of grey, intemperate circles—
like all lights, wounded and wounding.

You walked according to a habit
made of sound and bone and will.
Words edged, close-set as coral in your long line of days
where the white suns flowered like molars.

Your words now broken off,
mended, judged and dead,
and, the collectors say,
no longer wrong.

ABOUT THE AUTHOR

Patricia Nelson is a semi-retired attorney and environmentalist. She has worked with the "Activist" group of poets in California for many years. The group rose to brief prominence in the 1940s and 50s and is now undergoing a resurgence of publication by a different generation of poets. The Activist credo is that every word in a poem should be poetically "active," employing some kind of focused poetic technique—a principle not as self-evident as it might sound. The group often works with metaphoric imagery.

www.ingramcontent.com/pod-product-compliance
Lightning Source LLC
Chambersburg PA
CBHW022038090426
42741CB00007B/1111